A Dark Journey to a Light Future

THE TOMMIE MABRY EXPERIENCE

TOMMIE MABRY

Edited by Carlos D. Smith, Ed.S

WESTBOW
P R E S S®
A DIVISION OF THOMAS NELSON
& ZONDERVAN

WestBow Press books may be ordered through booksellers or by contacting:

WestBow Press
A Division of Thomas Nelson & Zondervan
1663 Liberty Drive
Bloomington, IN 47403
www.westbowpress.com
844-714-3454

ISBN: 978-1-4497-4056-6 (sc)
ISBN: 978-1-4497-4058-0 (hc)
ISBN: 978-1-4497-4057-3 (e)

Library of Congress Control Number: 2012902644

Print information available on the last page.

WestBow Press rev. date: 01/28/2021

Chapter 1:
LONELINESS

Loneliness is a terrible feeling. Not being connected to someone or something can truly destroy the confidence of any human being. This is especially true for a child.

I understand that man is not created to be alone. Therefore, my natural desire to be around people and be connected to them was quite normal. Yet, I missed this early in my life. Due to an overwhelming sense of loneliness, I attempted to connect to anything. Unfortunately, my solution to combating loneliness was not a wise one.

Happiness is hard to give, but easy to take

For the most part, I was a normal kid with normal childlike behavior. Along the way, I discovered the one thing that gave me a certain kind of thrill—the thrill of upsetting others. Or, as I would realize years later, the thrill of destroying things that made others happy.

I am the youngest of six children. I have an older sister, Francessa; two older brothers, Joe and James; and two adopted brothers, Chris and Roy. Life was tough growing up with five older siblings. I was able to wreak havoc on my siblings and essentially escape the punishment because I was the youngest.

I was closer in age to my sister than to my brothers. The large age difference made it hard to connect with my siblings. I was always viewed as a responsibility placed on them by my parents when they worked or slept, or as a pest when I just wanted to hang around them. I can hardly recall moments from my childhood in which I felt like a welcome sight to my siblings. They were very good at communicating how much of a burden I was to them.

However, I began to notice that they enjoyed playing video games, watching television, or hanging with friends. Everyone seemed to be happy except me. I decided to change that.

The first time I realized that I could influence the mood of a person was when my sister screamed for me to leave her room. Francessa had been relaxing with her friends when I decided to drop in. After all, she was having fun, and I was bored and lonely.

I didn't understand the concept that the girls were her friends only, or that I shouldn't be allowed to hang out with them.

Francessa soon made the rules of friendship and little brothers clear to me. The way she reacted by me simply walking in her room was incredible. I realized that Francessa felt the same way I did—angry.

I actually caused such anger! It was fantastic!

Naturally, I was destined to repeat this action again, not only to Francessa, but to the whole house.

No one seemed to understand my lack of happiness because they were blinded by their own. I don't believe I was deliberately being neglected; but for a small child, it certainly seemed that way.

The way I saw it was if I was unhappy, others should be unhappy too.

I began cutting the wires to my brothers' television and game consoles. I destroyed my sister's dolls and physically attacked her friends when they came over. I believed that if the things that made them happy were taken away, then we could all be unhappy together. At the very least, we could spend time with each other. Of course, that didn't happen.

Lucky for me, I began to develop a close relationship with my neighbor, Taja T. Martin. Taja was the girl of my dreams. She provided everything I wanted in a friend and a sibling. We were so close that our parents would joke about planning our wedding.

Time seemed to fly when I was with Taja. My siblings don't know this, but if Taja and I hadn't become close friends, many more of their belongings probably would have been destroyed.

My parents loved each other, but they argued frequently. I remember crying outside their door with my sister crying, because we heard my father beat up on my mother.

My dad wasn't the abuser type like the ones portrayed on television. My dad was hurt and angry that Mom was cheating on him. Mom would come in at all hours of the night; and once she did, the arguing began.

To outsiders, we seemed to be one of the happiest families.

My mom went to bingo every other night. Sometimes, we tagged along. At times, we stayed so long that we fell asleep on top of the bingo tables. We often stayed until the place closed.

Sometimes when my mom went to Bingo, she took the money needed to pay the household bills, which led to another fight with my dad.

It would hurt and anger me so much when my parents fought. I would shoot my BB gun out of my window hoping to hit somebody as they drove by.

All attention is not good attention

My parents worked a lot. They were gone early in the morning and returned late in the evening. They left my brothers Joe and James in charge.

I am twelve years younger than Joe and ten years younger than James. If I wanted to cross the line and do as I pleased, I hoped that Joe would catch me instead of James. James was the type of brother that gave an order and expected you to follow it. He carried the demeanor of my father, which made me respect him.

Being the youngest and so far away in age from my siblings, I longed for attention. I would run around the house making noise. Or I'd hide and destroy my sister's dolls just so she would chase me. My emptiness was not relieved until my dad came home because he gave me the attention I was craving. When he went back to work the next morning, I started in exactly where I left off.

By the time I was six, I had absorbed the name I had heard for so long—*troublemaker.* My brother Chris and I were close in age, so we sneaked out of the house and ran the streets while my parents were at work. We threw rocks into houses, shot the neighbors pets, and set things on fire.

All from boredom and a need for attention! While attending Casey Elementary School in the first grade, I became a teacher's worst nightmare. I fought daily and stole students' lunch money. I played tricks on the teachers just so I could make the kids laugh…things like putting glue in their desks.

By second grade, I had been suspended at least twelve times. It was so bad that a teacher told my father that if I were to return the next year, she wouldn't teach anymore. I knew that each time I got into trouble, my father would be called. Although he would be upset, I cherished the time spent being lectured. During those lectures, he asked questions and seemed interested in what was going on.

I was kicked out of Casey Elementary and placed into a program that was geared toward troubled youth. I was kicked out of that program, too.

By the fourth grade, I had been kicked out of three schools. Things were getting worse. By fifth grade, I had already attended seven schools, and my behavior was not improving. Chris and I began to hang around some older guys who began teaching us the ways of the streets. These guys gave me some of the attention I was craving. I was also happy to be hanging with Chris, who would become my partner in crime—*literally.*

I remember the first house we invaded together. We destroyed everything. We took anything we thought worthy of selling. We also stole bicycles. We swapped bike parts so that the victims couldn't recognize or identify their own bikes.

The first time I was caught, I broke into the state fairgrounds with four other dudes. The police caught us and took us to jail. I was only in the fifth grade!

For my dad to see me in a jail jumpsuit hurt me so bad, but it didn't stop me. He said, "So this is how you want to spend the rest of your life, living behind bars?"

I told him *no*, but I was laughing because I felt life was a big joke. I knew that since I was young, I would get out. The judge told me that with my attitude, I would be dead or locked up in five years. I said *okay* with a grin on my face. Little did that judge know after he released me the next day, he had created a monster within me. His words fueled a fire inside that was already burning.

During that time, my parents were going through a divorce. The family split up. My dad took my sister and me. My mom took my brothers. It took a definite toll on me.

My mom started making trips to the hospital from stress-related illnesses. She was on the verge of having a mental breakdown. Then my dad started going back and forth to jail.

Before reaching my teen years, I was forced to deal with a lot of responsibility. My dad worked overnight, which left my sister and me to keep the house in order. She would cook and clean and try to be a mother to me. My sister and I both ran the streets at night because no one was there to tell us not to. Words cannot express how much I missed my mom.

I met an older guy named Timmy, who reminded me a lot of my father. He had a strong personality, and he gave me attention. I found myself wanting to be just like him. He introduced me to another group of guys that became my family. Timmy showed me what family could mean for me: acceptance and attention.

I was hooked all the way. Timmy also had tattoos and gold teeth. Although I was not told to get those things, I wanted them because Timmy had them.

I received my first tattoo from a guy on the streets. My tattoos brought me the attention I craved.

All I ever wanted was attention.

Chapter 2:

EXCITEMENT

Excitement is a word I often read about, but hardly ever experienced. I had the thrill of causing harm to others, yet I never truly felt excitement.

These days, I define excitement as an enlivened anticipation. Excitement is like a cold, not as common, but something to be caught and passed along.

It's surprising how easily excitement can be passed to a child. A child can catch excitement when they notice someone caring about them. A child can catch excitement when they realize someone loves them. Or when they believe someone believes in them. I think every child should catch excitement at least one time in their lives.

A recognized passion can bring joy

My father built a basketball court in the backyard, and we played on teams while my mom cheered us on from the kitchen. My father became hard on my brothers about sports. My father hadn't gone as far as he wanted in sports because of his pattern of going to jail.

My brothers pushed my sister and me really hard in sports. They believed in beating us up to make us tougher. I would play them all night without winning one single game. Like our father, they pushed us so hard that they instilled a hunger to win.

When my brother James was in high school, he played basketball and was very talented at it. I wanted badly to follow in his footsteps. He took me to practice with him, which is how I learned the game. Unfortunately, he dropped out of school and started working to help out around the house. He was very smart, but he felt a responsibility to earn money.

On the other hand, my brother Joe was always an honor-roll student. He also had a strong passion for music. I used to sit by his door and listen to him rap all day and night. He sometimes allowed me to rap with him.

Regrettably, he was kicked out of school for having a fake gun in his bag. The sad part is that someone put the gun in there behind his back. This killed his confidence in human faith and trust. He dropped out and got a General Educational Development (GED).

My brother Roy was the kind of person who would steal everything around him and take anything he wanted. He was not a bad person necessarily. He just didn't see the benefits of doing things right. He was a different breed from the family and a natural loner.

My brother Chris was almost the spitting image of me. We shared similar interests in competing, fighting, and stealing.

My sister hung out with all five of her brothers because she didn't want to be left out. She developed a knack for doing hair.

I knew I could always go and play basketball when times were hard. I was not the average basketball player in the hood. I was exceptionally good, and I was always taller and had more skills than the people in my age group. Chris and I would go to the courts and play older people for money because we knew they would bet high. They didn't think someone my age could beat them.

Even though I was not as smart in the classroom, I was very talented on the court. Some of my friends told me I could go pro if I changed my focus from the street. I just laughed because that was not my style back then.

One of the boys in the hood whom we all looked up to when it came to basketball was Monta Ellis. He was our age and really good at playing basketball. Nobody could stop him. I had another friend named Chris Smith who was into basketball also. He played on *Heat*, a city league team coached by Coach Carrel.

Coach Carrel always asked me to come and play with them. I always refused because it didn't make any money for me. Besides, my image had changed. I had another agenda.

I had finally come up with enough money and enough courage to beg my parents to allow me to get two gold teeth. They wouldn't agree for the first hundred times I asked until I showed them how much money I had saved from what they thought were allowances.

They finally agreed on two conditions. The first condition was that I had to do well in school. The second condition was that I had to promise to play city-league basketball. I agreed to both conditions.

I would have agreed to anything to get those gold teeth!

When I first got my gold teeth, it was amazing to me. Both of my parents had them. They made me promise that I wouldn't grow up to be like them because neither of them had finished high school. Even though high school was far away, I promised them anyway. I didn't care if I lied to them because everyone around me lied.

One day while I was at the park playing basketball, Coach Carrel drove by. He stopped and approached me saying, "Boy, you are really good. Have you ever thought about playing on a team?"

I asked him, "For how much?"

He laughed, but I was serious. Then I remembered the promise I had made to my parents. I said, "Yeah I'll try it out."

My first game was crazy. My father was there, and he was bragging on me to everybody. It was crazy because he believed in me and I didn't!

At the tip off, the referee stopped the game because the parents on the opposite team protested that I was a thug and too old to play on a twelve-and-under team. With my height, gold teeth, and tattoos, I looked older than anyone else. They said I couldn't play until I brought a birth certificate to the next game.

I threw the ball and said, "My hood is waiting on me!" and I walked out.

My dad ran and grabbed me and said, "Red, it's going to be all right. I'll get you a birth certificate for the next game. Just don't give up because of how society makes you out to be." I said *whatever*, because I felt rejected.

When the next game day came, I was armed with my birth certificate. I took it to the referees. They were shocked to see that I was only twelve years old.

I had so much anger in me, which motivated me to score thirty points. In the opening game, I was doing things that kids my age couldn't do. I was already dunking the ball, which shocked everyone in the audience.

They were looking at a kid who looked like a thug, yet they recognized how much potential I had. At the end of the game, I walked straight to my Dad because he had been quiet the whole game. I said, "Dad, what's wrong?"

He said, "Red, I never knew you were that good." He had tears in his eyes. For the first time in my life, I was proud of myself because I had made my dad proud.

From that day forward, I was known as a superstar thug. Every game, people came to see me dunk the ball. No one believed that someone as young as I could dunk. Every time I did it, the gym went crazy. I gained a name for myself on the court and actually began to feel good about myself.

Positive support offers glimmers of hope

One day I was stopped by a guy driving a new Delta '88 with rims. His name was Curtis. He said to me, "Little man, I like your style. What side you claim?"

As usual, I said "North Inn."

His response was, "Do you know you're in West Jackson?"

I said, "Yeah, I put on anywhere."

He said, "Boy you have heart." He told me what he did for a living and asked me if I wanted to join his *family*. I turned his offer down until he said the money would change my mind. I asked what kind of money he was talking about. He told me to hop in his car and ride with him. I began to put my bike in his trunk when he said, "Leave it. You won't need that anymore."

We pulled into a place that resembled a car shop. He explained to me what my job would be. I would steal a car and bring it in. I'd receive a hundred dollars for each one. He taught me how to steal a car and crank it without using the keys. Basketball and school went to the back of my mind—money was the only thing in there now.

He reassured me that I'd be let go if I were to be caught because I was so young and in school.

By the first week, I had about a thousand dollars. Although the money was great, it also scared me. The money I had before never compared to what I was receiving now.

I would sometimes drive to school and couldn't wait for the other kids to see me driving. At that time, the only people who had cars were the teachers. I was not even old enough for a driver's permit.

It was easy for me to sneak around because my father worked from six in the morning until eight at night. He never had eyes on me until he came home from work.

School was only two minutes away. I'd go to school and act up each day until I was sent to In-School Suspension (ISS) or the principal's office. I just hoped that the principal would suspend me, but he knew that was exactly what I wanted him to do. I would fight just about everyday simply because I believed people were jealous of me. I found any reason to attack my school or classmates.

By November, the school was having basketball tryouts. Word had already gotten to the coach about me. He knew I was on the city league team, and he saw me playing during gym period. He was also the one who kicked me out of the gym everyday because I was cutting class. I never wanted to be in class because I thought I was too cool to do the work. Besides, I felt as if I were dumb and that my grades had already proven that.

I never wanted anyone to laugh at me. I didn't want the teacher to ask me a question or make me read anything. What

I did love was making the girls laugh in class, so I always pulled pranks. I threw paper at the teacher or got up and hit people while they were trying to work. I made fun of anyone that seemed smart.

I thought it was smart to be dumb, and dumb to be smart

I also cheated and slept in class. The teacher would call my father and he had to leave work to come get me. He would beg me to try out for the basketball team. He knew that when I was involved in something positive like basketball, I would stay out of trouble. Plus, to play basketball at school, I had to maintain certain grades.

When my report cards came out, I had all F's and an A in gym. The fact that I couldn't play didn't bother me because I had weekend games with my city league.

I looked forward to the weekends so my father and older friends could come out and support me. As my fan club increased—and my father continued being proud of me—basketball became more and more fun to me. All of that made up for what I did or didn't do in school.

I knew school was not for me. I realized I was in love with the streets. The streets paid while school and basketball didn't.

Basketball was more important to me than school simply because that was where I gained so much support and heard so many people cheering me on.

My name traveled so fast that I started playing Amateur Athletic Union (AAU) basketball for several different teams. Each week, a different coach would call my dad asking if I could play for them. Coach Alexander of our rival team, the Wolf Pack, called me and He told me I had the heart of a champion.

My body was becoming covered with tattoos I was getting a tattoo almost weekly. They were tattoos of things that I believed in and stood for.

Coach Alexander taught me a lot about the game of basketball, which made my talent grow stronger. However, basketball wasn't showing me the kind of money that I wanted. I was eager to make more money, and jail didn't worry me. I thought of jail as a joke.

My dad would ask where I got certain clothes. I told him that my friends gave them to me. He would say, "What did I tell you? You don't have any friends.

I was eager to make more money, so I went to Curtis and asked him to explain the drug business to me. He explained that it made a lot more money, but it was a more dangerous risk. He said I could really do some serious time for selling drugs.

I didn't care.

My father wasn't able to watch my every move, but I still knew I had to dodge him. Even though I was *bad*, I was still scared of him. I would tell him that I was going to my friend's house. He often said *trouble is easy to get into but hard to get out of.* I would casually agree and leave the house, staying out all night just to make a dollar.

Drinking and smoking wasn't a big deal to me. I just did it to feel older. I hid my intoxication by bathing before I came home.

My seventh grade year was coming to a close, and my basketball team was ending for the summer when I received a call from Attorney Chokwe Lumumba. He was a very important man.

He told me that he had once represented rapper Tupac Shukur. Then he got down to business by telling me he had a traveling basketball team—the Jackson Panthers.

I didn't understand what a traveling team was since I'd never been outside of Jackson, Mississippi, with one exception. Once, my mother took us all to the beach. I managed to get us kicked out of the hotel because I tore things up.

I didn't feel like I was ready to leave Jackson again!

However, Mr. Lumumba explained that the Jackson Panthers traveled around the world and competed against some of the best basketball players in my age group. I told him to let me talk about it with my parents to see what they thought about it.

When my dad got home, I told him. Naturally, he was happy. He knew who Mr. Lumumba was and saw it as a great honor that he'd called me.

Even though my mother and I were slightly on bad terms, I still talked to her on the phone regularly. I was supposed to visit her and my family that following weekend for the first time in a while, so I figured I would tell her then.

On my visit over the week I found out my sister was pregnant. She'd dropped out of school and moved to my mom's place. My brothers, Chris and Roy, had already quit school. I was the only sibling still in school.

When I saw my mother, I immediately ran and gave her a huge hug and she cried tears of joy. I told her the news about my basketball offer. She was so excited. She knew Mr. Lumumba and thought it was a great idea. She believed my staying busy would keep me out of trouble.

My family and I had a lot to catch up on, so the first thing my brothers and I did was head for the basketball court. They were all shocked at how tall I had gotten. I was 6'1" and just thirteen years old!

When we stopped playing, they sat down with me and had a serious talk. They explained that I was the last hope to make it in the family. They didn't want me to fail. I told them I would make it for them.

I have to admit that I was not as serious about it as they were.

When summer came, I went on my first trip with the new team. We traveled to Little Rock, Arkansas, to play in a big tournament name *Real Deal on the Hill*. It was an amazing experience—my first time riding on a charter bus, and my first time meeting all of my new teammates. I only knew a few of them from playing against them in previous games. We had players from all over the state.

The hotel where we stayed was huge. Each room was filled with shoes, wristbands, and bags with our names on it. All eyes were on us when we walked into the gym. Everyone started clapping.

It turns out; the Jackson Panthers was a well-recognized traveling basketball team. People were ready to see us play. That was something I had never experienced.

We won our first game, and I scored twenty-five points. I was signing my name on shorts for kids around my age. The coach from the opposing team told me that he had not met a guy with my kind of potential in a very long time.

Because of family issues, our regular coach didn't coach us our first game. Mr. Lumumba coached us, which was fine with me since he was the owner.

I was so excited when we finally got to meet our coach. Mr. Lumumba called a meeting at the hotel to introduce us.

When the new coach walked in, my eyes got huge! I knew him from the city league. He'd coached a group named the Dream Team. The Dream Team always won. I was scared of him because he always yelled at his players on the court. He was a stern coach who believed in discipline. He introduced himself as Coach Lemond Roy. I was really shaking because I was standing in front of the best coach around.

Once the meeting was over, he asked everyone except me to leave and get some rest. I was terrified. I thought about how I used to talk smack to him while I played. He was more than aware of my attitude on the court. I usually got kicked out of the game for cursing or throwing the ball down.

What would he say to me?

It wasn't what I expected.

He started out by telling me that he was the reason why Mr. Lumumba had called me. He knew I would be a good fit for the Jackson Panthers despite my attitude and tattoos. He said he saw greatness in me and that he appreciated the heart I had to win.

Believe me, I was not expecting this!

When I walked away, I knew that we shared one thing in common—the desire to win. Coach Roy and I hated to lose.

When I went back to my room, I immediately started a pillow fight with my roommate. I was still excited to be away from home. We messed up the room and went down the hall waking the other teammates. We threw ice down the hall. We were having a great time until the front desk attendant called the coach and complained that we were making too much noise.

When Coach Roy came out of his room, I was standing in the hall holding a bucket of ice. He screamed at us to put our shoes on and meet him outside.

It had to be around 2 o'clock in the morning. Everyone but me went outside. I told him I was not going anywhere, and that he was not going to yell at me like that. I told him that he needed to show me some respect.

He grabbed me by the neck, and we fought until I finally gave up. He said, "On this traveling team, you're going to respect me and any other grown up. You're not in your hood so show some character."

I felt as though he had *played* me. I was mad, but I went outside anyway. Coach Roy made us run for what seemed like forever and threatened to send us all back home if it happened again.

I went back to my room fuming. The whole night I thought about him grabbing me. I wanted to fight him even more, but I was enjoying the trip too much to make trouble.

The next morning we ate a huge breakfast at the Waffle House. Nobody was talking. We were all still scared from the previous night.

I was a little nervous to play for this coach, because I knew he would yell at us the entire game.

At tip off, I got ready to walk onto the court when the referee ran out yelling, "This old man can't play with these kids!"

I told him I was thirteen, and this time, I could prove it. To play on an AAU league, you had to have your birth certificate. Luckily, my father made me take mine, and I was able to prove my age without any problem.

By halftime, we were up by three points. We were all laughing on the way to the locker room. Our coach came in yelling, "What's so funny? We're 100 points better than them!" he said.

I said, "Coach we're doing the best we can." He responded with, "If that's the best y'all can do, then we're going home now!"

Everybody knew then that we had to give a full 100 percent to please Coach Roy. We went back out and won by fifty points. He hollered at each position until we gave him our best effort and our last breath. He played me the entire game. When I got tired, he pushed me to keep going.

I gained so much respect for him. Not only was he hard on the court, he was firm on us off the court. From that day forward, when I was around him or in public, I was scared to misbehave. I focused on showing good character.

On the way back home, Coach Roy asked me to ride in front with him. He explained that the reason he was so hard on us was that he wanted to make men out of us, not just basketball players. He said if I gave him seventy-five percent on the court, he wasn't going to play me. He explained that anything less than 100 percent would be cheating me. He wanted me to give my all, even when I was exhausted or ready to give up.

I enjoyed that kind of tough love because it reminded me of my father, except Coach Roy was tougher than my dad .In that one weekend, Coach Roy showed me something that I would carry with me forever.

I was so ready to get back home to tell my family and friends about my trip and experiences. While I was away, I never thought about my neighborhood, friends, or anything else—just basketball.

When Coach Roy dropped me off at home, he told me to be ready for practice at five a.m. because we were leaving for another trip on Friday. Instead of questioning or complaining, I just said, "Okay!"

My family was extremely happy for me when I told them about the trip. Part of their joy was that none of the family had ever been out of Mississippi.

I was proud of myself. I was the youngest kid in the family, and I would be getting on a plane to go back out of town later in the week. I had never been on a plane before, and neither had anyone I knew at the time.

That summer I traveled every week playing basketball and forgetting about everything back at home. I met a lot of new people. No one in my neighborhood had ever been out of town. This was not only a new experience for me, but also for everyone around me.

By the end of the summer, I had been to eight different states playing basketball. That was the most basketball I had ever played. We played at least three games a day. The entire summer passed without me getting into trouble.

Now that was truly remarkable.

At school, all I did was think about playing basketball on the weekends. I also couldn't wait until the following summer so I could travel again.

Chapter 3:
ANXIETY

When one is accustomed to living a certain way or has been doing something for a long time, the idea of change can be scary.

Fear can lead to anxiety, which can sometimes cause us to make unwise decisions. I realize that my anxiety for achieving greatness resulted in many moments of failure.

I was nervous about a new future. Actually, I was nervous about the idea of having a future. I had always lived in the *right now*. Where I grew up, tomorrow was not a guarantee.

> ### *Instead of telling me what I can't do,*
> ### *try showing me what I can do*

My hate for school was still alive. On my first day of the eighth grade, my dad told me before he left for work to start

25

strong with a new beginning and try to change my behavior and grades. That way, I could play basketball for the school. He said the same people that laughed at the jokes I made would be the same people going ahead while I was still making jokes. He kissed me on the forehead and told me he had a surprise for me later.

The first day of school was the first time I was able to hang out with my boys in a while. Since I was gone the entire summer, they accused me of getting *soft* on the streets.

I had to show them I had not lost it.

At lunchtime, I spied a boy in the lunch line counting his money. I told my boys, *watch this*. I ran toward him and punched him. When he hit the ground, I took his money.

I was suspended from school. My dad came to school mad. That was the first day of school, and he had just spoken to me about not getting into trouble. He took me home and told me to stay in my room. My pockets were empty, and I was ready to start making money on the streets again.

My dad later came in my room and told me to come to the living room. He had a surprise for me. He wanted me to meet a lady he had been dating for a few months.

She introduced herself as Tiki Jenkins. She wasn't my mother, so I didn't want to like her.

She had several college degrees. My mother hadn't finished high school, nor had my father.

Surprisingly, she turned out to be nice. She showered me with attention and gave me everything I wanted or needed.

On the other hand, she was very strict and detailed about everything. She made me say *yes ma'am* and *no ma'am* to her. I even had to say *yes sir* and *no sir* to my dad. It took me a while to catch on, but I finally accepted it.

She showed me a lot of love, which started wearing my defenses down. She never complained about how bad I was or about anything that I had done. She finally moved in with us. Believe me, I didn't mind. She treated me like her son.

She was dead serious about school. She actually made me do my homework and checked my weekly behavior and grades. Although I was getting into trouble every day, she didn't give up on me.

When Chris and Francessa visited, they loved her as soon as they met her. They each had their own room, and she showed them the same love she showed me. Now that she was in the house, she encouraged my dad to stop allowing me to go outside late at night. That was when I began not to like her as much. In a way, she cared too much. Her love and care was interrupting my money flow.

Despite their best efforts, I still went out all hours of the night. One night I was getting ready to go out and make my normal runs when I heard my dad and Ms. Tiki arguing. She was angry with my dad for allowing me to do what I wanted.

My dad just wanted me to learn from my mistakes. He didn't believe in whooping me every time I did something wrong. He talked to me every day and explained life to me. His method was to give me the forewarnings about things with the hopes that I would make the best decision.

In my opinion, he knew that correcting me wouldn't solve anything—I was still going to do what I wanted to do. Besides, he couldn't watch my every step.

The only thing I had going for me was hustling and playing on my city league basketball team. School basketball tryouts were around the corner and again my grades were awful...so awful that I hid my report cards for weeks.

Ms. Tiki called the school to see when they were releasing the grades, and they told her that report cards had gone out weeks earlier.

When Ms. Tiki finally saw my grades, she exploded.

She took me to school the next day and complained to my principal that the teachers were not doing their jobs. They were allowing me to sleep, cheat, and be kicked out of class. Then they passed me to the next grade at the end of the year.

Ms. Tiki put an end to that by threatening to sue the school if they just kept passing me on without me learning anything.

I continued to stay in trouble until my school finally had enough. They warned me that the next time I got into trouble, I would be kicked out.

The year passed and I managed to stay out of trouble. However, my grades were not getting any better. I concluded that I was just dumb like people said I was.

As my eighth grade promotion day approached, everybody was proud because I was heading off to high school.

My family arrived at the graduation ceremony with balloons. I was joyous knowing how proud they were of me for graduating to the ninth grade.

I was also excited because summer was just around the corner, and that meant playing basketball.

When my grades were sent home, Ms. Tiki was the first to see them. She frowned as she looked at them. Hardy Middle School had retained me in the eighth grade. I felt so bad. My family had been so proud of me. Now I had to tell them that I didn't pass.

I had become use to the school just passing me to the next grade. Then I remembered Ms.Tiki threatening them about doing that. I was so angry that my goal was to give every teacher at Hardy Middle School problems when I went back.

My father's voice kept playing in my head—*those kids who are laughing at you will move on while you're going to be in the same spot.*

That's exactly what happened.

I didn't let the situation bring me down because the summer meant more traveling. I was now fourteen and was placed in the 14-16 year-old bracket with the same coach. The schedule would be more advanced, and I'd have to play against high school students. My skills definitely had to elevate.

My first trip of the summer was to North Carolina. We played on the same court as Michael Jordan did when he was in college. That was so amazing to me.

For the first time, I thought about college, even though it was just a passing thought.

We won our first game and lost the second—which took us out of the first tournament. That experience was exactly what I needed.

We left North Carolina and flew to Houston to play in the Kingwood Basketball Tournament. We won the first two games and later won the championship game.

Although I was happy about my experience, I was a little sad at the same time because our next trip was not for four more weeks. That left me with nothing to do.

I went back to hanging with my boys. One of my friends had gotten his driver's license, which meant I could ride around the city with him. We rode around all night drinking, smoking, and visiting girls.

Around this time, a new skating rink opened for teenagers. It had the same atmosphere as a party club. We would drink and smoke the entire night and then go inside and have fun. When it was near closing time, we would start a fight just to be cool. We became known for fighting, which made the police show us away every time we came around.

One Friday night before a basketball trip, we got into an altercation with a group of boys at the skating rink. A police officer hit my friend in the head with a flashlight. I got so upset that I ran up to him and screamed, "Why did you hit my boy in the head with the flashlight?"

I don't know why I did that, but the officer hit me in the

mouth and the head with the same flashlight and nearly knocked me out. It took me a long time to get up. When I did, my head was throbbing and the inside of my mouth was busted.

I missed the trip the next morning because of a severe headache. That hurt me so bad because I had been so excited about going.

The first day of school finally came, and I was very embarrassed to be there because everyone knew me. I figured that I could try something new because I was older than everybody. I had a chance to look smart for a chance. I tried doing my work. Since I had nothing to lose, I began making a little effort. As the weeks passed, the basketball season came around. Once again, I couldn't play.

I was getting tired of school to the point that I wanted to quit before I even reached high school. What kept me from doing that was the disappointment it would cause my family. Although my behavior was still terrible, I was putting in more of an effort to do my school work. Unfortunately, I was still disturbing the class and making the entire class laugh until the school finally kicked me out for good.

I transferred to Siwell Middle School in South Jackson. Ms.Tiki and my father weren't happy about having to move to South Jackson. When we pulled up to our new house, I started smiling right away. The previous owner had left two basketball goals with a court in front of the house. That meant I could work on my game every day!

My father would come outside and play basketball with

me since I hadn't met anyone in the neighborhood yet. He encouraged me and told me how good I could be if I would just do better in school. He wanted me to go further than the people around me.

I didn't believe I could do that. I had been kicked out of every school I'd ever attended. Everything I had touched turned sour. No one wanted me to stay in their house. I felt lost. The only things I had were basketball and my family.

Not knowing anyone in my neighborhood, I was lonely. One day some guys came walking up the street bouncing a basketball. They asked me to play.

When they saw me play, they were amazed. They told everyone in the neighborhood that I was a superstar. Everyday someone new asked me to play against them.

After the Christmas break, I started my first day at my new school. Everyone already knew who I was—word from the neighborhood had spread.

The kids there loved me. They thought my basketball skills, tattoos, and gold teeth were all cool. The teachers, of course, had a different perspective of me. One of the teachers told me in front of the class, "Tommie, you will never make it in life with the image you have. No job will hire you." He also told me I wouldn't make it past high school.

It made me furious when I heard remarks that I wouldn't amount to anything. Every time he handed out a test, he said, "I know Tommie isn't going to pass, so I don't even have to grade it."

The kids thought it was funny. I just thought it was embarrassing.

One day at home listening to music, I was in bed reciting lyrics to a song word for word. Then it hit me. How could I learn new lyrics to a song in about a week, but couldn't remember anything I learned in school? Maybe I wasn't as dumb as I and everyone thought.

Right then, I made up my mind that my priorities were in the wrong place. A switch turned on. From that day forward, I tried to learn my schoolwork as I did my music.

After that, things went well in class because I focused and studied. I started passing all of my work but still wasn't making As. I was doing just enough to get by to prove that teacher wrong.

As the year progressed, I improved. I knew I was on the right track for graduating this time.

When graduation came, my family was skeptical about coming because of the experience from the previous year. However, I passed and moved on to the ninth grade.

The summer began with us traveling to Orlando to play. At our first game of the summer, there were college scouts looking for talent. I had never played in a gym with people writing down my every move. That made our first game extremely intense. Everyone was competing for spots in college and the NBA. I knew I had to step up my game.

That was the first time I pictured myself playing in front of fans in a university. I met players who later went on to play in the NBA.

It was everybody's dream to get a free ride to college... except for me.

After the game, I met a coach from the University of Arkansas at Little Rock who told me I had a future in basketball. I was curious about what he meant by a future, and he said he meant a future in which I played college basketball. I thought he was joking, but to my surprise, he was serious. He told me in order to play college basketball I had to hit the books hard. Thank goodness that wasn't a problem at the time because I was trying to do better. He never said anything negative about my tattoos and gold teeth. I felt a little better about my image.

That talk with the college coach drastically changed my mindset.

When I traveled, my focus was not on the streets or on selling drugs. As soon as I returned home, I went right back to the same old things.

I was now at the point of trying to figure out at which high school to play ball. My AAU coach was friends with the coach at Bailey Magnet High School in the heart of the hood. I say that because all of my friends from the North Inn attended that school. It was also a very challenging school.

When I met the coach, he explained to me that my image was not a problem but it was crucial that I did my work. I considered that a win-win situation because I was able to get back with my friends and break the cycle in my family of not finishing school.

I can't walk in my future with my foot in my past

When I was about five years old, my siblings and I were home alone watching television. All of a sudden, we heard the doorknob turn as if someone was trying to come in. Two men dressed in black broke the glass and began forcing their way into the house. We were scared half to death!

We sneaked out the back door to our neighbor's house to call the police. They never came.

They probably got those calls day and night. Did that give them the right to ignore us? Of course not. We were still humans whose lives were in danger.

That incident gave me one of my first insights into life, and the understanding of how society perceived the people who lived in our kind of neighborhood.

Now, about to enter high school, I had to overcome the feeling that I was doomed. I felt like I had lost so much prior to coming to high school. I believed that my experiences from my early childhood would be repeated or were indicative of what would happen to me as an adult.

Earlier in my life, I had a great friend named TajaT. Martin. In my heart, I yearned for her to be with me experiencing the first day of high school, as well as my success with AAU.

That would never happen. Taja was taken from me by a drunk driver.

I never forgot the day a frantic phone call came from my sister. She was crying hysterically. She told me that Taja was rushed to the hospital and that she'd been hit by a drunk driver. Taja and another girl had been riding a go-cart when the drunk driver ignored a stop sign and hit them.

I didn't know what to expect. I just knew I needed to get to the hospital to get to Taja.

By the time my dad and I made it to the hospital, everyone was in the waiting room crying. I ran to the back to see Taja. I saw her mom on the floor crying. I grabbed her and told her it was going to be fine. I felt like Taja would bounce back, and we would be talking on the phone again. Her mom told me Taja had died instantly.

I hit the ground. Nothing in the world could have ever prepared me for that. I cried and cried. My mind was so overwhelmed with grief that I hated to talk to anyone for a long time. I didn't want to get close to another person ever again. I couldn't stand feeling that type of agony again.

That had been six years earlier. Although I believed I wouldn't survive such a tragedy, I did.

Recalling the pain of that incident, I was filled with the belief that surviving that kind of pain made me strong enough to survive high school.

So, in a way, Taja *was* still helping me.

On the first day of high school, my dad and Ms. Tiki explained that God was doing something with my life. My dad told me to surround myself with positive people. Ms. Tiki told me to show respect to my teachers and get into the habit of being respectful to adults. She wanted me to practice what

I had learned at home. This was the first time I really took a different approach to school.

My teachers saw all of my tattoos and gold teeth and pre-judged me. They didn't know what I had been through or what I was going through. I started seeing how my previous image was hurtful to my future.

To counter it, I showed so much respect, they went out of their way to help me. They started smiling when I came around. I never felt so good around people before.

My confidence was building so much that I started making a good impression the first time I met someone. It helped me get through my issues. The teachers loved my attitude toward school.

I met some guys at school who were as *bad* as me, but they had less experience than I had in the streets. They knew me as a good basketball player, but my street credit was something they wanted to know more about. They started to look up to me.

At school, I did enough to get by with Cs and Ds. Because I was a little older, things were somewhat different. I could go places and hang with older girls. I started getting more tattoos. My habits of drinking and smoking were increasing daily. It seemed to be great fun to get out of class and ride around high and drunk. The difference was that the people I rode around with all had their drivers' licenses and their car weren't stolen.

The basketball season tryouts were approaching, and I was excited. I'd been waiting for that chance. My grades were just good enough to try out for the team.

The first day of tryouts, the varsity players tried to haze us by making us carry their bags and talking down to us about our skills. They told us not to try out and to stick to the Junior Varsity team. I knew how good I was at basketball, so the hazing caused me to develop a bad attitude. No one actually liked me on the team.

As tryouts continued, they noticed that my talent was unusual for a newcomer. Varsity members saw me as a threat to their positions on the team.

The coach informed us he had no time to waste and already had his team picked out. What he'd decided was to keep all of his old players and two new guys. I was one of the new guys he picked.

I was excited to tell my family what happened. When I told my dad, he was beyond happy for me and said that my future started right then.

At that moment, I didn't understand what that meant.

Our coach had to leave before the season started. That hurt me deeply, because now I had to start over with a new coach. When the new coach came, everything changed. He viewed me as just a ninth grader who had room to grow. He favored the older people and would sit me down in practice and tell me to watch the older boys and learn from them. That pushed me to the limit. I would cuss and argue with him the entire practice.

I couldn't understand why I couldn't be on the first or second practice team. He always put the older boys out there so that they could work on their game.

Nonetheless, I was still the only one who scored. Quitting came to mind a lot, but I knew that's what other people expected me to do. I also had the voice of my middle-school teacher in my head telling me I wouldn't amount to anything in life.

Those two things actually changed me. I took all of that negativity and used it to build my confidence.

Bailey was known in the state as being the underdog. I was excited to play in our first school game. My dad, sister, cousins, and friends came to support me.

We started losing, and I was stuck on the bench, something I wasn't use to. By the second half, I was really upset. I kept asking my coach to put me in the game. He told me to wait my turn and that my time was coming. I was double angry because my family and friends were there to support me.

We lost that game by forty points. I felt like giving up on school. I was so mad, I cried.

When I got into the locker room, everyone was laughing. I flipped out. Losing was not my style. I walked out of there with my head down, listening to the cheers of the other team and hearing the down talk of our team by our peers. Some people thought I was a sorry player because I wasn't put into the game.

My sister was sitting with my dad, and he was as upbeat as ever. He told me he was proud of me no matter what happened. He said I had accomplished so much by just being there and that my time was coming. I walked with him to the car feeling depressed.

Each game was the same—I wasn't allowed in the game. Though I didn't get to play, my dad and sister were always there supporting and encouraging me. I was getting frustrated with this because I wasn't shining like I wanted to. I started hanging out late with my friends, and they told me I should just quit and make money.

My focus started shifting from basketball to the streets again.

One night, I was with some friends when one of my boys asked me to go up the street to the store with him. About halfway there, I realized I had my gun on me. I told him I was going to run it back to where we'd come from. On the way back to the store, I heard tires squealing and five gunshots. I ran up the street and saw my friend lying on the ground covered in blood.

I had just been with him! That could have easily been me! I couldn't believe so much could happen in a split second.

We rushed him to the hospital, but he died. I couldn't get my mind around the fact that we had just been laughing and talking thirty minutes earlier. Now, my friend was dead.

The whole night, I dreamed of how that could have been me. I later found out that my friend had shot at the boys who did the drive-by a few weeks earlier when I was at a game.

What killed my friend was a retaliation.

I thanked God for watching over me and turning me around for that spilt second.

That turned my focus back to basketball. I started noticing

how all of my boys from the past were fading away from me—they were either locked up or dead.

When we came back from the Christmas break, I met with my coach to explain how much I wanted to play and how good I was. He knew how good I was but thought of me only as a practice player with room to grow.

Our season was almost over, and we were winning a few games, but not enough to brag about. At least I was proud of myself for my grades and for still being on the team.

The playoff game started off. We were losing and our boys were getting into foul trouble. Some of our fans were leaving. Everyone was losing hope. By halftime, we were down 29 to 39. In the locker room, I stood up and yelled, "What's wrong with you guys? We're only down ten and y'all are ready to give up. We're forty points better than that team."

I said that in my summer league coach's style. Coach said, "Tommie is right."

That shocked me, but not as much as when he told me I could start off the second half!

I trotted out onto the floor, and my dad stood up and cheered. The whole gym was excited.

My first shot was a three pointer, and I made it. Everybody went crazy! I was so geared up and ready. I went to the basket with no problem. I played hard on both sides of the court and got my players involved. They went at it.

I ended the game with nineteen points, and we won by five. I felt so good. My coach looked into my eyes and said he couldn't believe it. My teammates were jumping on me, and my dad was running around the gym. It just felt so fantastic.

For the first time, I saw my name in the morning paper. People were calling and giving me congratulations.

Although we lost the next game, I had finally made a name for myself as a freshman. I told myself after the last game we played that I would work very hard the coming summer. I set some goals to be captain of my high school team the next year and determined ahead of time that we were going to win games. I set my goals and standards so high that I wanted to do whatever it took to reach them.

My grades were good enough for me to pass to the tenth grade. My focus for the summer had shifted far more than I had expected. I approached it with the attitude that it would be my last year playing AAU basketball. I had so much to prove in my next basketball season that I knew I had to get better.

When I returned home from the AAU trip, I found out that my high school coach was being replaced with someone new. This was very shocking to me, because I had tried so hard my previous summer to make my mark on him and the new team.

Now I had to start over again with a new coach with new ideas and concepts.

Coach Speech, our new coach, called a meeting with the returning players.

Right off the bat, the coaches explained to me that they knew who I was and that I was the future. Their comments built me up and made me realize that I had a lot to live up to. I immediately loved them for recognizing my talents and all the hard work that I'd put into my game. I put my best foot forward the entire summer and worked my hardest to improve my game every chance I got.

The first day of tenth grade was perfect because we were national AAU champions. I had regained my respect back by taking my talent to the national level. My teammates were also excited because they knew I could help them win. I started hanging with my teammates so I could build a family-like bond with them.

I felt like I was becoming a real leader.

Because of my basketball achievements, the state of Mississippi put me on the "to watch" list, which was a Scout page in the newspapers allowing everyone to view the best new players in the state. My name was becoming more popular every day.

It was getting to the point where my friends from the hood were becoming upset with me, but that didn't matter. I was on a mission to make my goals come true.

Going into my first game of the season, I was in the starting lineup. I was only in the tenth grade, yet I was the captain. The gym was packed. I was more than ready. The difference with this game was that I had to start right since we were playing a rival school team that we had lost to the previous year. There was no way I was going to let that happen again this year.

Starting from the tip off, we led the game, which was a shock to the fans. I played like it was my last game. We won, and I ended with twenty points.

It felt so good to beat that team in the first game!

After that, we started beating teams that people thought we couldn't beat.

My father was so proud of me he bought me a car. He figured if I had my own car, I wouldn't have to ride with friends he didn't trust.

Unfortunately, I felt as though no one could tell me anything. I would drive around all night and still be able to drive to school the next morning. It got to the point that I would start leaving school early. My coach sometimes caught me and made me come back to school.

The teachers loved me, even though I had a thug appearance. They knew I had a good heart. My family was also proud of me. They enjoyed opening the paper and seeing me in there for some achievement.

One of my supporters was a teacher who was also the cheerleading coach. She found out that my nickname was Red, and she added on to it by calling me *Hot Boy Red.*

That nickname spread fast. At every game, they chanted *Hot Boy Red*, along with a cheer that the cheerleading team made up.

My friends from the streets always came to support me at my games, so I felt as though I couldn't stop hanging around them. Also, I didn't want them to see me as a weakling.

For the most part, everything was good around that time. I had friends, a little money from my side hustles, and I was averaging twenty points a game. Because of the support of my whole family and my friends, I pushed myself to perform even harder.

Playoffs were right around the corner. It felt extremely good because the team was good enough to go far into the playoffs. I wanted to win for them and compete in the championship because my school had been in the playoffs just once since it was founded. I set a goal to play in it before I graduated.

But that's not what happened.

We lost. Our season ended short.

The remainder of the school year, I worked more on my basketball skills and hung out more.

In the middle of the summer, I received a letter from Southeast Louisiana to play for their college. It was amazing to realize that colleges actually wanted me.

As the summer passed, I received more and more letters. After every game, I saw my coach talking to the college scouts about us. That changed my focus. Now I wanted to play harder so I could go to college. Time was moving on, and I only had two more seasons left at school.

My teammates and I stayed up late a lot of times talking about playing against one another in college. It felt so good to actually dream like that. Going into my junior year, I was extremely motivated. I was in the top twenty in Mississippi for my junior class among hundreds of teams. My goal was to make *the Danny Dozen*—the top twelve players in the state. That was every player's dream. Monta Ellis was drafted into the NBA right out of high school, and Jackson native Moe Williams was already in the NBA, which opened doors for all basketball players in Jackson Mississippi. Seeing a childhood friend drafted like that gave me the hope and encouragement to attend college.

As a junior in high school, I wanted to get really involved in the activities at school. I had been hearing about prom since I was in the ninth grade; but at my school, only juniors and seniors could go to prom.

My stepmother spoiled me since I was finally on the right track. She rented a really nice car for me to ride in. I also ran for Prom Prince to represent the junior class males.

My school friends and I arrived at the prom together and were the main attraction. Everywhere we went, people noticed us. I was shaking as I waited for the announcement of who won the title as Prom Prince. When they called my name, everybody started screaming and cheering for me! I felt more famous than I had ever felt before.

We were scheduled for basketball practice at five a.m. the next morning, and all of my teammates went home early. I didn't. There was no way I was going home early. I had already been drinking, and I had a new car. I wanted to continue partying.

I teamed up with some of my older friends and got extremely drunk. I proceeded to get involved in a fight with some guys at a store and got into an argument with a police officer. He took us to jail for the night but released us later the next day.

My coach was furious with me. I apologized to my team and to the coach. I refocused and continued on with the season.

The season was getting good and teams were playing their best against us. I was also playing my best trying to reach my goal of getting to the tournament. During the playoffs, two of our star players were injured. That led us into losing again.

Fortunately, I had one more year to reach my goal of winning the playoffs. Word had gotten out that I would make *the Danny Dozen* list the next season. That inspired me to work even harder after the season and into the summer. My last year of playing was coming up, and I knew I had to make a mark and make it my best season.

I earnestly played my hardest that summer to prove to the college scouts that I wanted to play for their schools. I was getting letters of interests but no offers. Then a coach saw me and told me that he had been watching me since my ninth-grade year. He told me he'd seen how much I had matured as a person. He offered me a full scholarship to play for Alcorn State University.

That was huge, and I felt all of my work had paid off.

When my family heard the news, they went crazy. My mom called all of our relatives. Not everyone believed what they had heard. I had some relatives who were excited, but I also had some that didn't have faith in me. They viewed me as a thug and considered my family and me a waste of talent.

Hearing those negative things made me very upset. I never thought of my family as a waste of talent. That put me on another mission to prove society and those relatives were wrong. No one else was motivating me at the time except for my family, so I had to learn how to motivate myself. I had to continue to tell myself that I could do it. I had to gather all of my negative thoughts and turn them into positive ones. I felt as though if I were to fail, it would prove society and the others had been right.

The coach at Alcorn told me in order to attend a four-year college I had to take the ACT. I had never heard of it before. I was pretty nervous because I wasn't the best test taker. Actually, I had always cheated on my tests, or did just enough to get by.

More offers came in, but I was told the same thing about taking the ACT. I realized I had to get more serious about my priorities and set my goals higher than I had ever done before. After all, my family was depending on me. I couldn't let them down.

The first day of my senior year, my dad told me, "This is your year. Have fun with it, but watch the crowd you hang with. The smallest thing can cost you everything that you've worked so hard to get."

He spoke from his heart when he told me that, and I felt it.

Everyday was as though I was living a life that was just

too good to be true. It was far away from what I had ever imagined. I was almost waiting for something to kick me back into reality.

I didn't have to wait long.

One day I was sitting in my car before I drove to school when I received a phone call from one of my friends. He told me that everybody was going to skip school and chill. I was a little taken back because I was the one who usually called the shots. I agreed and met up with the guys.

We were all sitting around outside when I heard gunshots. We were shocked. I looked down and saw a hole in one of my boy's shorts. Soon after, I started feeling very weird. I had been shot in the foot accidentally.

One of my friends rushed me to the hospital. He called my dad and told him I had been shot. The x-ray results showed the bullet lodged an inch away from causing me to lose my entire foot. Then the doctor delivered the worse news ever—he wasn't sure if I could move my foot properly enough to play basketball again.

That news hit everyone in my family extremely hard.

Because I had skipped school to hang with friends, I had jeopardized all the things I had worked so hard to have. I never thought that something so unbelievable would ever happen to me.

My dad carried me home and laid me in the bed. That was one of the saddest moments of my life. Everything seemed to go downhill from there.

The doctor placed me on bed rest. That meant I couldn't be nominated for *the Danny Dozen*. That broke my heart all over again. I couldn't do anything but cry.

I just kept asking God *why me?* I began to have nightmares about getting shot in the chest and just hearing those infamous words of my dad on my first day of school all over again.

I continued to stay in bed crying and praying to God to get me through and grant me a miracle. One day, Dad came in and told me that I couldn't just sit in bed and feel sorry for myself. He reminded me that doctors could only tell you what they believe medically, but if God had other plans, nothing could get in the way of that. I just had to have faith.

I absorbed every word.

From that moment on, I started walking around on my crutches. It came to me that only a handful of people had been around to visit me. That made me decide to hang around just the people who had my best interests in mind.

About three weeks after the accident, I started waking up at five every morning and training myself with any exercise I knew. The school basketball season was coming up, and I was determined I was not going to let the doctor tell me that I couldn't play.

In the meantime, I'd sit and watch my teammates practice and just cry.

I kept striving and working so much that I started walking and could even run a little bit. My dad ordered a boot for me to put inside of my shoe to help me balance. I went to practice;

and although I looked strange with a big boot on my foot, I was hungry to get back on the court.

My coach kept telling me *no* and I kept saying *yes* until he allowed me to do as much as I could. My teammates thought I was crazy, but they were excited at the same time. By that time, I had been gone for almost a month.

The day before the first game, I got *only the strong survive* tattoo on my arm and *God is good* tattoo on the side of my neck. I had overcome obstacles that no one could believe I would live through.

Before the game, my Dad came to me in tears and asked how I felt. I told him just watch and he would know. I told him how much I loved him and thanked him for believing in me. With so much anger built inside of me from all of the negative assumptions that people had of me and my family, I was more than ready for this game.

I came off from the start scoring my first ten points. Although I was in pain, I thought of it as only mental, and continued on. Everybody—including me—was shocked. I ended the game scoring thirty points.

Even though we lost, I thanked God for allowing me the strength to pull through.

Soon after, I began doing strength training with my coach . I knew I wanted to go to college and there was no more room for just sliding by.

I was determined to be a leader, and I wanted my grades to

prove that. I found out something—I wasn't dumb. All I had to do was apply myself.

My first report card was full of As, Bs, and one D. I made it my mission to turn that D into an A.

A celebrity guest speaker, actor and comedian Tommy Ford from the sitcom Martin, came to put on a program at our school. He asked for a volunteer, and I was the first to run up on stage. When the program was over, I asked him if I could have five minutes of his time to talk to him. To my surprise, he agreed.

I told him a little about my background and asked for some advice. He told me something that has never left me. He said, "Never use your background as an excuse for not succeeding. You can be whatever you want to be if you put forth the effort."

That was huge to me. He inspired me to soar to higher heights with a vision in mind. I began to believe that I couldn't be denied anything if I just kept my goals in sight.

I wanted to follow in Mr. Ford's footsteps. He was so influential to me, I wanted to give back to kids who were younger than me.

I felt God steering me in a different direction. I started volunteering around town and speaking to the youth. They looked up to me and understood my image. They loved the positive advice I shared with them.

I wanted to catch kids before they headed down the road I had been on. If they were already on that road, I wanted to help them get off it.

Prom season of my senior year came, and I ran for Prom King. I wanted to be the first to win two years in a row. This year I had decided to bring a date. My eyes were on Valencia Rice, NFL Star Jerry Rice's niece. Fortunately for me, she agreed.

This year was going to be different. I wanted to have fun without the problems that I had my previous year. We walked in when they were about to announce the winner of Prom King and Queen. With half of the school's votes, I won. My queen was my last year's princess.

We enjoyed the night, but I made a different decision this time. I took it in real early to avoid trouble and continue to focus on my basketball season.

Playoff season approached, and my foot had gotten into great shape. We won the first game of the playoff. Each game was tougher. At last, we were one game away from going to the championship.

The next game came around, and we started off poor. We were down seventeen points at halftime. It looked as though our season was coming to an end, but, unbelievably, we came back and won!

I lay on the floor in shock. My dream had finally come true. I thanked God for bringing me through that dark road.

We lost the next game, but we were still going to the championship tournament.

Even though we lost the first game of the tournament, we gave it our all and were still proud of ourselves.

That was my last game of the season and the last game of my high school years.

I was nominated to play in the McDonald's All American game—a great honor. My high school years were over. Now I needed to hear from a college.

Thankfully, Missouri State University West Plains (MSU) called and asked me to come and play for them. They were a nationally ranked school, so I was excited to go. Being a junior college, I didn't need a certain ACT score to attend, which made me even more excited.

Although I wanted to go to a major four-year school, I was still thankful and blessed to be able to have a full scholarship to a two-year institution.

Signing day was a huge day and one I shall never forget. Who would have ever imagined someone with my appearance and background would get a full-college scholarship? And this after people telling me that in five years, I would either be dead or in jail. Adding to my joy was the fact that I was the first in my family to go to college.

I finished the final semester of my high school year and couldn't wait to walk across that auditorium stage and break the family cycle of dropping out of high school.

After the ceremony, my family members ran and gave me big hugs. It felt like we had all graduated that day.

The next week, I was on my way to MSU to take a few summer classes. I thanked my family for believing in me when no one else had—not even me. I had made new family history, and I wasn't finished yet.

Before leaving, I wrote out a goal:

> *I will do whatever it takes to succeed, and I*
> *will always shoot for above average.*

I felt like a new Tommie Mabry. I was going to college. Even though I was used to traveling, it was a little different now that I would actually be moving away. I packed up everything I owned and kissed my family goodbye.

Chapter 4:
FEAR

I'm not sure a person can truly be fearless. I think we can suppress or ignore the fears but that doesn't make them go away. Even with the life I had led so far, I found out that I could still experience fear.

I had lost several friends to the streets. I had lost my best friend. My parents had divorced. I had been shot. I had majorly struggled in school. It was natural that I was fearful of taking this next step in my life.

Fear made me reflect on my successes. I came to realize that fear could be fought with confidence, and that confidence will win.

Fear of fate can distract the vision of success

MSU in West Plains, Missouri, was six hours from Jackson, Mississippi. In those six hours, I cried every time I thought about what I was doing.

I was driving to college.

As I drove, I felt the presence of God riding steering me the whole way. It was another miracle.

It was very comforting to know that my dad and stepmother were behind me literally and physically. They were determined to see me succeed.

Entering West Plains, I immediately sensed that there were no black people around. I didn't see one black family. I felt like I was in the wrong place. Did I really want to be there? I wasn't accustomed to being around so many white people. I had nothing against white folks, but it was going to be a culture shock. Would my image intimidate them?

I pulled up at the local Wendy's restaurant, and everyone was excited to see me. The kids immediately ran out to get my autograph. They knew I was there to play basketball, and they were all so friendly to me.

I hated that I had misjudged them. I had always been a victim of being stereotyped and here I was doing the same thing.

The team's assistant coach, who was black, really couldn't explain to us why more blacks were not there. He said we had nothing to worry about, that the people in West Plains were good people. He reminded us that not all white people were bad, just like all black people were not good.

Our head coach, Coach O, invited us to dinner to get to know one another. His family was so loving and kind. We all had a chance to introduce ourselves; and when it was my turn, everyone tuned in extra hard. After all, I had a body full of tattoos and gold teeth in my mouth.

I explained my life story to them. They couldn't believe it. I will never forget what Coach O's wife told me, "Tommie you're going to be something special. Just keep God in your life. You may look a certain way, but when you talk, you're a completely different person."

This experience showed me what everybody meant when they said one's first impression is everything.

The next day was the first day of summer school, so we didn't stay up too late. I was feeling good about my new environment and college. I appreciated the fact that I had a chance to overcome my past and take college seriously.

Walking into my first college class, I was totally shocked. This atmosphere was completely different from high school. There was no talking or playing. The class was quiet, and the students were working.

The teacher read through the lecture fast with no pauses. By the end of class, my head was spinning. My notes were indecipherable. She told us that our first test was at the end of the week. I had heard the lecture, but I couldn't write that fast. Nor was I used to taking notes at that rate of speed.

My first lesson at college was that it wasn't something to play around with. I didn't know how I would keep up with everybody else and maintain a good enough GPA to play basketball.

My next class went the same way, and I was frustrated that I couldn't keep up. I knew I had to make some changes, so I brought a tape recorder to class everyday and taped the lecture.

That worked. I made my notes from the recording that night. I was pleased with myself for thinking outside the box. By Friday, I was ready for the test.

The teacher told us to leave when we were finished with the test. That was something I definitely wasn't familiar with. I quickly realized that college teachers didn't make you come or stay in class. The choice was mine. A poor choice would cost.

I flew through my test and felt good that I knew the answers. I was the first one to finish, so I left to get ready for my next class and for our first workout.

I was scheduled to have two classes each day for the whole summer and workouts with my coach three times a day.

At practice, there were only five players who were going to be challenging. The others were not supposed to make it until the fall. I never worked that hard before. We lifted weights, ran drills, and scrimmaged. I worked out so hard that I fell out from being so tired.

I was shocked that college workouts were so strenuous. I thought about quitting, but it wasn't really an option. I was too determined to succeed.

Coach told everyone to go to the locker room to shower after the workout. Everyone except me. He told me to stay on the line. I didn't understand why. He ran me so much more by myself. Every time I asked why I was running, he would add more. When we were finished, he told me to follow him to his office. He showed me an email from one of my teachers.

That email was crippling. It said: *Tommie Mabry cheated on his first test, making a 94 on it. Please advise him that this behavior will not be accepted here at MSU.*

I read it with disbelief. I looked at Coach O. I told him that I might not look like an ordinary college student, but that I was very intelligent and that I didn't cheat. He believed me and emailed her back.

She asked him to send me back to retest. I rushed out of his office furious.

This time, I was given a different version of the test. She placed me by her desk and watched my every move. Just like the first time, I ran through the test quickly. When I looked up, she was crying. She said that she'd made a big mistake and had judged me by the previous players that she'd had in her classes.

She hugged me and graded my paper on the spot. This time I made a 96, two points higher than the first time.

**"Never let your eyes make your heart decision
or you will be mentally blind"**

The importance of not judging a book by its cover became more apparent to me through that experience.

Being a college athlete and student wasn't easy. On weekends, we went out searching for something to do. Everyone we encountered was friendly and wanted autographs. They loved basketball in West Plains. They invited us to their homes for dinner and treated us like part of their family. Anything we needed, they made sure we had it.

We didn't lack for anything. Coach assigned us adopted parents to help us, and I went to my adopted parents' house to relax during my free time. We went fishing at the river or sat around and played games.

If not with them, I hung out with my teammates or worked on my basketball skills. There wasn't a lot to do in town—not even a mall to go to.

The town had one nightclub called the Firehouse. Coach O explained that it wouldn't be safe to go there. He warned us about a small group of people who frequented the Firehouse who wouldn't be enthusiastic about seeing black people. He told us we could get in real trouble, but he never actually forbade us to go.

We went and made the best of it.

Grades finally came, and I had earned an A and a B. I was extremely proud of myself. To top the day off, coach gave us two and a half weeks to go home. When we returned, the entire team would be there.

He told us to have fun because due to our hectic schedule once the season started, he didn't know when we could see our family again. I took his advice and enjoyed spending time with my family. I enjoyed updating them on my life. I definitely enjoyed hearing about my family's successes as well.

While at home, something magnificent happened. I met a beautiful young lady. At the time, I had no idea how important this young lady would be to me and my success. Her name was Taji Dorsey. I knew she was special because her name was very similar to that of my childhood best friend. My life seemed to becoming together more than ever.

Back at school, we had three returning players from the previous year and thirteen new freshmen. That made a big class of new players. I could tell they were really good. I knew I would have to work extra hard because everybody wanted a spot on the team.

My teammates were all cool characters from different parts of the country. With them all being here, I knew I was going to enjoy college life.

Everyone had partying on their mind. We partied through the night. The next morning while I was preparing to go to class, I heard complete silence. No one was up and moving and preparing for classes. I started beating on their doors making them get up.

We had no one to answer to and no supervision, so I figured we had to act like adults ourselves.

Once when the coach gave us a Friday off, we decided to go out as a team. Walking into the Firehouse, we immediately stood out. We tried to stick to ourselves and not say anything to anybody. Coach had warned us that we weren't safe in that nightclub, but we had to go somewhere.

About an hour after coming in, a group of guys approached and asked us if we were in the right spot.

One of the guys pushed one of my teammates. Since we were family, we all got into a fight. Things went from bad to worse. We tore the Firehouse up. The owner kicked us out.

As we were leaving, a police officer stopped us. He said, "Our ball players do not act like this."

We couldn't explain what happened. The police officer called our coach. Needless to say, Coach O was furious with us.

As we prepared ourselves for the first game, things began to lighten up. Coach told us we were all capable of starting. He was going with the unit that played well together. Our playing time was based on how good our unit played. I didn't like that, but I accepted the rules. I knew my unit wasn't the strongest because we didn't play very well together.

Every time my unit got onto the court in practice, Coach O made us get off so he could try another unit. The day of the first game, people were lined up outside for tickets and autographs. I didn't realize we were loved that much. The whole town came out to support the team. The gym was packed to capacity. I felt like I was in the NBA!

News stations and reporters were there. Our pictures were

hanging up around the gym. The only thing I was missing was having my father at the game. At least he would be listening to the game on the radio at work.

When the game started, it sounded like the stands were about to collapse—the people were so excited. I loved it!

The coach went with the best unit to start the game. They quickly ran the score up by twenty points. I knew that wasn't good for my unit, but I was all about winning. My coach believed that if it wasn't broke, don't fix it. He kept that same unit on the court for a long time.

When the time came for my unit to substitute, we looked terrible. We had too many egos on the unit. Coach pulled us off and went with another unit. Even they were doing well. My unit watched from the bench. That made me upset, but I cheered my team on as we won the first game.

Inside, I felt like I was in the ninth grade all over again. We'd won a game in which I had a few brief minutes to play. The good part was that my dad got to listen to my first few minutes of college basketball.

For the next few games, we did the samething on the court, with the exception that my unit played better each game. We were on a ten-game winning streak and were the center of attention in town. My adopted parents went to the games to watch me play and supported my every move.

Things were going great until one awful day.

We were in the weight room doing a light workout just to stay fit. Lifting the weights on a standing machine, I fell to the ground in severe pain. I couldn't move or stand up. My teammates lifted me up and took me to the hospital.

The doctor told me I had pulled muscles in my back. Further, he didn't know how long before I could return to the court.

I couldn't understand why every time something good happened in my life, bad followed close behind it. I was afraid that my basketball days were over.

I couldn't travel with the team or attend class. A teammate brought me my classwork every day. I could barely take a shower and use the restroom. I couldn't even bend over to tie my shoes!

I listened to our games on the radio. That was a sad time for me. I wanted to keep it away from my family, so I told my dad I wasn't playing because of a problem between coach and me.

I felt hopeless. I couldn't accept just lying around. I prayed every night, begging God for a miracle.

The things I took for granted, I couldn't do anymore. Weeks passed, and nothing was improving. I went back to the doctor and begged him to do something.

The doctor told me there was nothing he could really do. He told me to keep resting. He also told me to ask my coach to provide a massage therapist for me and that it might help the pain. I told the coach, and he gave me the number of a massage therapist.

More weeks went by. I finally started seeing an improvement. I was beginning to be able to walk, bend, and even do a light jog. I prayed every day to keep improving. I thanked God for every improvement he delivered to me.

At last, I was able to go to the gym and watch my team practice. When the doctor released me to begin playing again, I was so far behind. However, I was thankful to be back.

My first game back, the fans welcomed me back by giving me a standing ovation. I knew my dad would be listening. The first play of the game, I got a steal in, went down the court, and dunked the ball—my first dunk of my college career. I didn't even think about my back. But when I came down after the dunk, it was hurting.

I played through the pain. Coach let my unit play the whole game. I ended the game with fifteen points.

Coach called the team in for a meeting to wrap up the season. He gave us the bad news that he wouldn't be coaching us the next year because he was taking another coaching job in another state. That was very shocking news. Our assistant coach was also leaving.

That was heartbreaking news because any coach that replaced them would more than likely bring his own players. Since I'd been hurt half of the last season, it would be hard to get signed to come back.

With my next year not being promised, I had to at least keep my grades up and pray that I could find somewhere else to play.

As a team, we tried to get all the time in with one another before we left. None of us knew where we would be the next basketball season.

We decided to go back to the Firehouse for one last time. I told them no because I had a funny feeling about it. They still wanted to go and enjoy our last days, so I let them talk me into it.

It would be a night to remember.

As soon as we stepped inside the club, I felt a bad vibe. I tried to stop the team one more time, but they ignored me. I regretted that I hadn't gone with my first instincts and stayed away.

A group of guys watched us the whole night. After a girl came over for an autograph, the group of guys started moving toward us. I prepared for something to go down.

A guy threw a beer in my face. One of my teammates grabbed a bottle and smashed him over the head. The fight was on!

It lasted about five minutes before the police came.

My teammate's head was bleeding. We rushed him to the hospital. I was infuriated with myself because I hadn't stuck with my initial uneasy feelings.

The doctor stitched our teammate up, and we headed back to the dormitory as mad as could be. When we arrived, the police was waiting on us.

They asked especially for me since a witness identified me as the guy with the tattoos and gold teeth. I was blamed for starting the fight.

It wasn't my fight! We were merely in the wrong place at the wrong time.

The police arrested me. I really hated myself because it all could have been avoided if I would have just stayed at the dorm that night.

The good news was that I was quickly released for lack of evidence.

Back at home in Jackson, I lived by the phone, praying and hoping for a call. I didn't have a clue about my future.

The call I was waiting for came from Coach Doug of Lawson State in Birmingham, Alabama. He had heard about what happened at MSU and had also seen me play. He wanted me to sign to play at Lawson State.

He had also attended the game in which I got my first dunk. He was there recruiting a guy from the opposite team but said he could tell my back had been hurting. He liked my endurance.

Birmingham was just a few hours from Jackson and was also a junior college. He offered me a one-year scholarship. He'd also signed two of my teammates from MSU: Carlos Collier and Anthony Hurvey.

I was more than happy to sign up!

Coach Doug told me the dormitories were over-crowed and that we'd have to find our own apartment. I had no money to pay rent, and I knew my credit wasn't good enough to sign an apartment lease.

Right away, I began calling everywhere close to Lawson

State looking for a job and an apartment. Everybody told me my credit wasn't good enough to sign a lease. It was really stressful not having a job or a place to stay.

In the meantime, I started going around town working with the youth to try to give back to the community and share some of my wisdom with the kids. I wanted to share how great God was treating me and I wanted to encourage young people to keep hope alive in their lives. I started booking my own speaking engagements.

It was almost time for school to start and I still hadn't found a place to stay. My mother told me that if it was God's will, an apartment would be waiting on me when I get there. I had nothing to lose, so I left for Birmingham. I kissed my family goodbye—again—and headed to Alabama.

Never use the situation around you as an excuse not to succeed

In Birmingham, I met Carlos and Anthony moving their stuff in. I asked Carlos, "What you doing man? You found a cosigner?" He told me no, he'd just come to town with the same mindset as I had. He said the apartment manager just gave him the key and asked him for his first month's rent.

I met the apartment manager, and she told me the same thing. That was good news but still a major problem. I didn't have enough money for the first month's rent with me.

I had no choice but to call my parents and ask them to send money. They sent the money without hesitation.

I later found out that Coach Doug had arranged the apartment situation for us. I felt a tremendous load lifted off my back. I thanked God for making a way.

We moved in and got directions to the college, which was thirty minutes away. I hated to have to drive thirty minutes every day going back and forth to school. All the other players stayed in the dormitories. Anthony, Carlos and I were like outsiders.

At the gym, we noticed a certain vibe. We walked in looking professional with our basketball bags and wearing our practice gear. Since Missouri State had more money to support their athletic department, we had nice stuff. We soon found out that Lawson State was different.

Coach Doug met with us for about half an hour and explained to the other players that we were coming to take a spot on the team. He wanted the other players to improve their game, but they took it to mean that we were better. Our previous ranking placed MSU above Lawson State.

Right away, we noticed the players keeping their distance from us. Plus, we were the only three players not from Birmingham.

Like always, we introduced ourselves. When it was time for my introduction, everybody was looking at me as if I were from another planet. When I finished, a guy stood and asked me how many tattoos I had and if my gold teeth were real. I replied truthfully by telling him and the team that I had fifty-four tattoos and that my gold teeth were real.

Then everybody wanted to ask me different questions about my life. They had never seen a player like me. At the end of the questioning, coach explained to them that I had the highest GPA on the team. They were astounded to hear that I took my classwork seriously.

Here I was again—having to change preconceived notions of who I was.

Because classes started the next morning, I knew we had to complete our move into our apartment rather fast. I also wanted to get some good rest.

Anthony and Carlos had different plans. They met up with some girls from school and invited them over to the apartment. I heard them partying all night while I tried to get some sleep. I guessed I couldn't be mad since this was their place, too.

Next morning, I walked into the living room and saw everyone sprawled out on the floor. Beer bottles were everywhere. I started yelling, and they woke up. I told them it was all right to have fun, but school came first. I made them get up and go to class.

It took a few weeks before the team began vibing with us. Once we invited them over after practice for a barbeque, things went pretty good on the court after that.

The second month's rent was due, and I didn't have any money or a job. I talked to coach about working at the school doing work-study, and he gave me a job doing paperwork for him.

Since I was now living in a neighborhood that resembled

mine back home, I decided to get involved in the community. I volunteered at schools to speak to the kids about my life. I was hoping I could inspire them to succeed past any roadblocks that they were facing.

I was dead serious about my speaking engagements. Any time I had free time, I made it my business to go speak to kids. I started giving out season tickets to the ones who wanted to see me play. It felt great to give the kids a chance to see a college basketball game.

Our season opener loomed closer. My basketball abilities were at their best, and my back was in good shape. The whole night before the first game, I tossed and turned. I couldn't wait for that big day to come.

When the game started, the whole gym was packed with fans and television reporters. As the ball tipped off, I glanced at the door and saw my family and Taji walking in. I could tell they were excited to see me.

First play down the court, Anthony passed me the ball. I shot a long three pointer and made it. The gym went crazy. My family was jumping up and down with joy. I was just too happy.

Unfortunately, we lost the game. I had a season opener of twenty points, Anthony had nineteen points, and Carlos had fifteen points. We were not happy with the fact that we lost. We loved winning. Points didn't mean much if we didn't win.

As the season went on, we were becoming more famous around town. Everywhere we went, people called us *the Big*

Three. Things couldn't be any better. My grades were good—I had all As and Bs.

With no Cs, I was on point with everything until certain players started having meetings with the coach against *the Big Three.* They felt they should be playing the same time as us. Their dislike for us started to show in the game. Certain players avoided passing us the ball. The team started to break up, and we started playing poorly. That caused us to lose games on a regular basis.

Coach had to do something, so he switched the lineup. He took Anthony and me out of the starting lineup and decreased Carlos's playing time. The other players started playing better. That wasn't a shock. They had all played together the previous year, so they had good chemistry.

It all seemed so familiar—everytime things were going great for me, something happened. I became agitated because we were being treated unfairly for no other reason than jealousy.

Basketball was beginning to frustrate me. I started to second-guess if it was even for me. I knew I was good, but I was tired of the same thing happening to me. If it wasn't an injury, it was some type of conflict that prevented me from playing. My focus for the game started to shift.

Barely getting to play, I stopped going to practice. My relationship with the coach eroded. He fired me because I also stopped going to work. That made things worse. It all became too much for me. I didn't have a job, which meant I had no money to pay my rent. Plus, word got out that coach was talking to the athletic director about revoking my scholarship.

Anthony and Carlos were on the same page as me. They later quit the team too. We felt as if we had been mistreated.

Eager to find money for my rent, I did something I told myself I would never do again. This time I was stopped dead in my tracks.

I knew some guys that lived by me in the apartment who sold drugs. I asked them to connect me with their boss. They gave me his number, I called, and we talked for a while. He asked me to meet him at a gas station to talk in person.

The whole way there I was thinking about something going wrong. I really didn't want to do it, but I felt it was my only option. I arrived at the gas station and parked. When I looked out my mirror, I saw the police pull over the car that I was supposed to meet. I pulled away so they wouldn't connect me in any way. As soon as I started to roll, another police car pulled me over. I was scared.

The police officer asked me if I was with the guy they had pulled over. I told him no. He saw my phone on my lap and asked for it. He called the last number in my phone, and the other guy's phone rang. He told me to get out the car for lying to him. At that point, I put my hands on my head and started crying. I knew I'd made a big mistake.

Just that fast—I had ruined my life.

The police officers told me they had been looking for the drug dude for a long time. He had enough drugs in his car to get sent away for a long time. I told the police officer I didn't know the guy and that I was just trying to get a CD from him.

One of the officers recognized me from playing basketball for Lawson State. He told the other officer to let me go, that I was a good person and a basketball player. He also asked me for an autograph for his son. Afterwards, he told me to be careful with whom I communicated with.

I was relieved but furious at myself because I had gone against my conscience. God had brought me out of another situation. I immediately thanked Him and called my coach to apologize. I also begged him for my job back and my spot on the team. He graciously allowed me to return. I was able to end the season with my team.

Thank God for being in control…as always.

With the year coming to an end, I had one major problem—Lawson State was a junior college. I had to find a four-year college. I hadn't received any college offers while at Lawson, so I knew it would be hard to find someone to give me a scholarship. I was good enough to make anybody's team; I just had to do some research.

I finished up at Lawson State with all As and Bs. I packed all my stuff and headed back to Jackson. I had no idea where I'd go the next year.

I had been in this situation before. I had faith that God would make a way for me. I said a prayer and got ready to see my family.

A lot had changed back home. My father and stepmother had divorced. My sister had another child. My mother had been moving from house to house. Chris and Roy moved to St. Louis, Missouri. James and his family were doing fine. Joseph was doing well in college.

I called to see which colleges around town might need me—I wanted to bring my talent back home. I also looked forward to my family getting to attend my games.

I received two phone calls from two coaches; one from Belhaven College, and the other from Tougaloo College. I was willing to sign with whichever college made the first offer.

Since both colleges were known for their intense academic programs, I was in a win-win situation.

My first tryout was with Belhaven College. The minute I walked in the gym, I felt like I was not supposed to be there. I had a funny feeling. Nonetheless, I had to win over the coaches because I really needed a scholarship. The coach put me on a team and told all of us to play a five-on-five game. Three coaches watched us.

Everything went bad. Every shot I took, I missed. I was falling down a lot. The other players were stealing the basketball from me. I couldn't believe how terrible I was performing. I knew I was better than this.

I could see the disappointed expressions on the coaches' faces. My high school coach had come to support me. He asked me if I was all right. I felt good. I couldn't explain why I wasn't playing well.

When tryouts were over, the coach met with us. He thanked us for coming, but said he couldn't use us for his upcoming season. I felt horrible because I had always made every team I'd tried out for. I was very upset with myself because I didn't get to show the coaches my talent.

Coach Lafayette Stribling, from Tougaloo College, was my last hope. He invited me to come for a try out. I had to make a good impression because Tougaloo seemed like my last chance.

I had heard a great deal about Coach Stribling, so it was exciting to get the opportunity to meet him. He was well known for winning at his last college, Mississippi Valley State University.

The minute I drove through the Tougaloo gates, I felt the vibe that this school was for me. When I walked into the gym, I smiled because I had such a good feeling about this place. I looked at the ceiling and saw the championship banners hanging there. Tougaloo College's basketball team was the defending champs.

Tougaloo had so much history. It was a private, historically black liberal arts institution founded in 1869.

The history of the college was so intimidating to me, but I made myself forget how badly I had played earlier and just focused on playing well for Coach Stribling.

Like Belhaven, I was placed on a team and played five on five. I was doing amazing things on the court. It was so weird, because everything I accomplished I hadn't been able to do hours earlier at Belhaven.

Coach stopped the game and offered me a full scholarship for my remaining two years. I quickly signed the acceptance offer and rushed home to tell my family. It was big news because Tougaloo was a very expensive college, and now I had a full scholarship to attend.

I was slated to go to a prestigious institution on a full scholarship! Yes, God was definitely in control.

Chapter 5:

HOPE

Hope is a wonderful thing—a glorious possession and a magnificent gift. I was overwhelmed with hope. Hope was all over me, in me, and through me. I was a big mass of walking hope.

Did I have hope five, ten, or fifteen years earlier? No, but I had it now, and I definitely wasn't going to lose it.

In proving society wrong, the sky is not the limit

My new scholarship opportunity was fantastic in another way, as well. I would be about ten minutes away from my family, and they could come to all my games.

Coach Stribling gave us the team rules. He explained that all his players were to stay in the same dormitory on the same hall. He said a team that stays together, plays together.

He also explained to us that we had to go to church with each other every Sunday.

What made this team amazing was that half of us already had college experience. We had talent that we could bring to the team.

Coach made all of the players attend the college freshmen and new students' orientation week. Anywhere one player went, the whole team had to go to support. It was a real family.

During orientation week, the Greek-lettered organizations sponsored lots of events on campus. People were barbequing and hanging out. There were different activities going on all over the campus.

I had always seen college life portrayed like that on television. Now I was right in the middle of living my dream of attending such a college. That's when it hit me! God had planned the whole thing! I was supposed to be at Tougaloo, not Belhaven.

The basketball team had its own hall in Berkshire Hall dormitory. My roommate, hall mates and I instantly became friends. A couple of the guys had a lot of tattoos. One of them even had gold teeth just like me. This was a very special group of boys. I met two players who shared many similarities as me, Mario Luckett and Otis Smith we hung out everyday.

I was having the time of my life. I decided to go to the gym to thank Coach Stribling again for allowing me to be there. When I got there, I met the Athletic Director, Dr. James Coleman; his assistant, Eric Picher; and the assistant coach—

Harvey Wardell. They were extremely nice, cool individuals. Dr. Coleman was my advisor since I was pursuing a degree in education.

I was really shocked to meet Dr. Beverly Wade Hogan, the president of Tougaloo. She turned out to be very personable and willing to interact with the student body.

After becoming acquainted with many of the faculty and staff members of the college, it was time to get serious about basketball.

Coach Stribling made me the captain of the basketball team, which was great since I was new at the school. He could have chosen any of the returning players. He said I had leadership qualities, and from the looks of my transcript, he said it was obvious that I took school seriously. The others players were really receptive of me.

We began intense training and conditioning sessions. We ran around the campus multiple times. Weeks passed, and we still hadn't touched a ball. Everything we did was outside. That was totally different from junior college basketball. It felt like the real thing.

Even though we worked hard, Tougaloo College kept us busy with plenty of fun activities. We enjoyed ourselves. The Greek-lettered organizations made the campus especially fun. They hosted events and performed stepping routines on campus. Student Affairs sponsored movie night on the lawn and late night cookouts. Sometimes the basketball team hosted dorm parties in our hall.

Even though I was living in Jackson, I barely left campus unless it was to go home or do community-service activities. However, since I was home, I could go speak at my old schools. Kids were starting to be a big passion for me—it was exciting to steer someone onto the right path. I knew I had the ability to lead and inspire others.

One day when I was doing community service, a guy told me about a lady named Ms. Gaynor. He said she owned a home school for kids who had been kicked out of school or who didn't do well in public schools. He said she had some students I might be able to help.

When I met Ms Gaynor, I knew she had a heart for kids. We talked for hours, and she asked me to be a mentor. After meeting the kids, one little guy stood out to me; his name was Joc.

Joc hated school. He had been expelled because of behavioral issues. He became my first mentee. I took him under my wing because he reminded me so much of myself when I was growing up.

He and I shared a lot of similar stories in the hood. I told him I would come see him every day after my first class. I had a desire to work with all the kids and show them a different path to choose.

Joc became a little brother to me. We talked on the phone about different things dealing with life. Anytime he had a problem, he called me. He told me he wanted to graduate from high school now since he'd met me. He also wanted to play basketball. I loved it that I was able to put a spark in Joc's life and get him excited about school.

I loved my world inside and outside of Tougaloo College.

Basketball season was about to start. The basketball team was the defending champs. We had high expectations. The student body hyped us up the whole week. They publicized the game around campus.

My family heard on the radio about our first game, and they—and Taji—invited everyone they knew. It was the first college game to see me play for some of my family. They really surprised me when they came to the game wearing T-shirts with my name on them!

The gym was packed with alumni and students. Tougaloo jumped out with the lead. We were up by twenty points before I knew it. Coach dropped players in as the game continued. Everybody contributed, and we won the game. The fans rushed the floor to congratulate us.

After the game, the student body threw a party for us on campus. That continued after every game, and we won lots of them.

The National Tournament was a great experience. It was designed like an NBA game. Our games were playing on large screens hanging from the ceiling, and the gym was packed. We went on to lose the first game, but we brought back a banner to hang up in the gym for making it to the National Tournament.

At this point in my life, I was humble and relaxed. My

basketball season had gone well, and I had everything I needed. I wished I had gone to Tougaloo College my freshman year.

I wanted to be involved with everything that transpired on campus. I was elected to be on the Teacher Council Board by Dr. Marilyn Coleman, the Dean of Education. My midterm GPA was a 3.1. I was also a tutor in my department. That was amazing because I once was described as a dummy.

Two positions the student body voted on were Mr. and Miss Tougaloo. The college took these positions serious because the elected individuals represented Tougaloo College as the king and queen.

To represent the college, Mr. and Miss Tougaloo had to serve as college ambassadors and be positive leaders for the student body.

The chosen candidates had to be well dressed and presentable. They had to have at least a 3.0 GPA, three letters of recommendation, a large percentage of student signatures, be a junior, and be active in student organizations.

Wouldn't you know it? I wanted to be Mr. Tougaloo.

I knew I'd have a hard time with one of the candidate qualifications. People liked me, but I didn't exactly look presentable to a lot of people with all my tattoos and gold teeth.

In my heart, I knew I had good intentions and that I was the perfect person for leadership. I met all of the other qualifications, so I didn't think that one obstacle should be too hard to conquer.

I didn't understand the type of trouble I was about to get into.

Make my tomorrow better than my yesterday

When the time came to get signatures, word had gotten around that a *thug* was running for Mr. Tougaloo. The people who knew me asked me if I was serious. My image had put a bad taste in the mouths of some of my peer's and some of the alumni's mouths. When people discovered that I was really serious, things went from bad to worse.

The criticism was heavy. It seemed as though I had done something terrible. I just wanted to make a difference and help others learn not to judge a book by its cover. I wouldn't have let Tougaloo College down for anything.

I started hearing rumors that the alumni didn't like what I stood for. I understood they didn't mean any harm personally; they just wanted the best for their college. I respected that.

However, people needed to understand me. If I were to be judged, I wanted to be judged on my intelligence and my ability to lead—not my image

How my image was perceived grew into a testy situation fast.

I received emails and letters that said things like; *get out of my school,* or *you can't be serious about running for Mr. Tougaloo with gold in your mouth and a body full of tattoos.*

Others said: *we will make sure you don't win,* and *you're a misfit of society.* Things were getting very bad, but it showed me how serious people were about my college.

I was receiving criticism from my peers, and the campaigning hadn't even started yet. I didn't understand what I had gotten myself into, but it was deep. I was not about to let this stop me from doing something I wanted to do. I was sure I had all the qualities of a good representative.

I hated how society stereotyped people. If God could forgive me, then everybody else should too.

I was ready to make history. Though it hurt to hear the rumors spread about me, it motivated me to push even harder. I was a person who had been given a second chance in life, and I now stood for success.

My campaign platform highlighted the four Bs:

Be motivated.

Be confident.

Be determined.

Be yourself.

I was absolutely ready to change the perception of who I was. I had to get everybody to see me as a leader. Being popular as a basketball talent and for how I treated other made it easy to get enough student volunteers to form my campaign team.

When it was almost time for the kick-off rally, all the candidates had to make a speech in front of the student body. That was my chance to explain why I was the perfect candidate. Already a motivational and inspirational speaker, I was ready to show the student body what I was all about.

The night before the big speech, I stayed up all night preparing my speech. I had to show them the real Tommie Mabry.

A lot of people gave me advice. Some of it was good, but some people wanted me to be something that I wasn't. I wasn't about to change who I was. I wanted to win by being exactly who I was. When I looked in the mirror, I saw a man, not a thug. I was happy with myself. My outer image merely represented my past struggles.

The day of the speech, I could tell how serious the contest was to everybody. The speeches took place in front of the student union. It seemed like the whole student body was there. That was the first time I saw my three opponents. They were well-dressed individuals, and they had all been at Tougaloo since their freshmen year. That presented another obstacle for me.

When I walked up to the podium, I felt everyone's eyes on me. This is the speech I gave that day.

Why I Am the Perfect Candidate for Mr.Tougaloo College?

I am the perfect candidate for Mr. Tougaloo College because I embody the principles and qualifications it takes to hold such a prestigious title. As an athlete, I want to change the stereotype about athletes—the stereotype that athletes are jocks. Speaking for myself, I am not a jock. Although I am an athlete, I also value a good education, and I understand that it is the main reason for my presence here at Tougaloo College.

As an education major, I currently hold a grade point average above a 3.0. People may look at me and think *Why does this guy want to be Mr. Tougaloo College? He doesn't fit the description of a college king.* Well, I do fit the description of Mr. Tougaloo. Mr. Tougaloo's main responsibility is to be an ambassador and role model for the male population at Tougaloo College.

As captain of the men's basketball team, I am a role model for my teammates. I encourage and motivate them to do their best—to never give up. With the slogan *Just Do It,* I hope to motivate not only the male population, but also the student body as a whole to just do whatever it is that they feel. Many times, our biggest critic is ourselves. In saying that, I have come up with the platform of the four Bs: Be Motivated, Be Confident, Be Determined, and Be Yourself. I will make it my duty to continue to motivate others to become motivated about whatever it is that they want to achieve in life. A lot of times, students are not confident with themselves, thus they never get to meet the real people they are. I want to show students how to be confident inside. Once you become confident in yourself, then you can be yourself and shine like the true star you are. I want to instill in the student body the fact that motivation leads to confidence; confidence leads to determination; and determination leads to YOU achieving your goals.

So you ask why I am the perfect candidate for Mr. Tougaloo College? I am the perfect candidate because I want to be the voice of the people. I want to help Tougaloo soar higher and reach the unreachable. I want the student body to *Just Do It*. Be Motivated, Be Confident, Be Determined, and BE YOURSELF.

When I was done, there was complete silence. I knew people were shocked to see how well I spoke. Then the applause came. That was the official start of my campaign to prove I could be Mr. Tougaloo College.

Every night I stayed up developing ideas. Every time I heard something bad about myself, I became more motivated to keep going. Some mornings I would wake up and see all of my posters pulled down and bad things written on them. I knew it was to upset me, but I was not about to entertain such foolishness. I was on a mission.

At the end of the week, we had one more opportunity to win student's votes. There was a Mr. and Miss Tougaloo Talent Showcase. It was a big event in which we had to model various types of clothing and show our talent. I really didn't have a talent to showcase on a stage besides motivational speaking. The only thing I could think of that would fit my lifestyle was rapping. I thought about the rapper, David Banner who was the voice of Jackson Mississippi and in my eyes he stood for something bigger than rap. He was a positive role model to the community as well. So I performed a rap that was well received, but it created another firestorm of negativity.

People from the other campaign team placed inappropriate things about me on various social networks. I had already become accustomed to the criticism. I didn't allow anything to get to me at that point. I was determined to win. I just tried to stay strong and have faith.

If I got down, I called my mother. She always reassured me that if it was God's will, I would win.

When Election Day came, I set up a booth in front of the voting site. I was so nervous I couldn't stop shaking. I watched every voter come in and out.

Around 5:30 that evening, the Student Government Association Advisor appeared. The place was packed with people wanting to find out who won. She read the Miss Tougaloo winner first Lateia Taylor. Then it was time for Mr. Tougaloo.

I don't mind admitting I was nervous.

The advisor announced there had been a tie between Mike Taylor and Tommie Mabry. I was extremely relieved to still be in the race. I had accomplished a lot so far, but things were about to get more intense.

We had very little time to prepare for the runoff since it was the very next day. I was even more nervous than before, but I had faith.

When I got back to the dorm, I saw papers under my door. One read, "No, we are not going to let your face go on Tougaloo College's website. Get serious."

Right after that, I read an email from an alum. It said, "I have watched you grow over time, and I want to wish you good luck tomorrow. I am so proud of you. Do not let anything get to you. You are a few steps away from making history. You are a winner in my book."

That email showed me that everyone was not against me. I was very encouraged by it. The truth is, I was never mad at the people who said bad things about me because they had a right to voice their opinions whether I liked it or not. It wasn't anything personal.

When it came to a position like king of a college, people wanted to be careful whom they voted for.

That whole night I wondered if I would win and how huge it would be for me to represent a college that people had once told me I would never enter.

The next morning, I set up another booth in front of the voting site and watched every voter come out. I couldn't believe so many voters turned out for a runoff between two people.

At 5:30 that evening, the results were revealed. The advisor said, "The winner is Tommie Mabry!"

My eyes got so big, and I fell to my knees and thanked God. I was making history.

This was an honor for my family. They had seen me go from hopeless to something special. My email inbox was full of people telling me how I had helped them get over the stereotypes. Those remarks made the outcome mean even more.

I completed my junior year not simply as Tommie Mabry, but as Tommie Mabry, Mr. Tougaloo College-Elect.

Over the summer, I thought about needing to put more into my classwork, which brought up the idea of quitting basketball and becoming more focused. That was a hard pill to swallow. I knew God was showing me a different route. Reaching out to people and being a mentor seemed to be my calling in life.

I had played basketball just about my whole life. Basketball helped me to get where I was, but it wasn't the only thing I knew how to do.

When I announced it publicly that I was not playing and hung my basketball shoes up, no one understood. My family was supportive, but I knew they didn't get it. My coaches told me to do whatever made me happy.

I figured if I couldn't give basketball a hundred percent, then I shouldn't do it. The NBA was not for everyone. I knew I only had one more year to play basketball, but making an impact on someone's life would last forever. I was ready to make that sacrifice. I couldn't ignore God's plans for me.

Tougaloo planned a trip for the student leaders to a retreat to learn leadership skills to bring back to the college. I was definitely ready to lead.

When school started in the fall, I felt weird not playing basketball. That was a first for me.

The first week of freshmen and new students' orientation, I spoke about college life. I could tell the freshmen couldn't believe I was really the campus king. Many of them asked me how I thought I could be Mr. Tougaloo with all my tattoos and gold teeth. I explained that anything is possible at Tougaloo College. I reminded them of our motto: *This is the college where history meets the future.*

I felt like a new man, so I wanted to try a new look. I'd always wondered how I would look without my gold teeth. I really had outgrown them. They represented my past. I wanted to take them out, but I knew it was very expensive.

I didn't have the money, so I prayed that God would make a way for me. As always, God answered my prayer.

Some weeks prior to school, I met with Pastor Dewayne Pickett from New Jerusalem Church in Jackson, Mississippi. I usually turned to him when I needed uplifting. He always took the time to help me stay on a spiritual path. I knew he would give me good advice.

I told him about my idea to take my gold teeth out. He thought it was a good idea and that he would pay for the work to be done.

Another huge blessing!

When the day came, I was scared that I might look funny since it had been over ten years since I had seen my real teeth. The process took a few hours. I was scared to look in the mirror. When I did, I couldn't believe how great my smile was without those gold teeth.

I was ready to show the world my new smile, an excellent way to start my senior year at Tougaloo College. My family was excited about it, too.

One day while traveling from a speaking engagement, I received a much-anticipated call. Joc called to invite me to his graduation. He said it was because of me that he finished school. What a powerful statement! I was in tears. I couldn't believe my words had been strong enough to change a child's life just as the leaders in my life had changed me.

After the ceremony, Ms. Gaynor called and asked if I would speak at a play she was presenting. She explained that she couldn't pay me, but she really needed me to do her that favor.

I agreed to do it. I needed money, but I couldn't be selfish. My words were God's words.

After I spoke at her event, another lady heard me. She asked if I would speak at her school, Whitten Middle School. She said the kids really wanted to hear my story. As soon as I walked in, I had the feeling that I was supposed to be there. I knew there were kids there that just needed a little guidance.

After I spoke, the principal, Anthony Moore, told me he was amazed to hear my story. He gave me his card and asked about my major and when I was to finish school. I told him that I would finish in a few weeks with a degree in education. He smiled and told me to call him when I graduated. Not thinking much of it, I put his card in my wallet and left.

When the big day came, I was totally excited. I never dreamed that I would be at MY college graduation. I was ready to make history again.

My seat was at the very front by the stage. It was a hot Mother's Day. What better gift to give my mom? What better gift to give my family!

The whole time I sat in my chair crying under my shades. I could do nothing but think of how far I had come. Now I was minutes away from hearing those blessed words.

The Dean of Education approached the podium and said words I thought I would never hear: "With a bachelor's degree in Education, with honors, Mr. Tougaloo College—Tommie Mabry!"

That was the million-dollar prize—the championship ring that had always eluded me. It was the overcoming of discouraging words from negative people. It was the blessing bestowed by God.

That degree represented a child who was never really told about college, a child who was talked about his whole life, a child that was now walking with a college diploma in his hand.

From being locked up, hustling in the streets, and being shot, I had just arisen above the earth and put my footprints on the moon.

Thank you God!

I walked across the stage, headed for my family, and collapsed crying in their arms.

After graduation, I continued to speak at events while I hunted for a teaching job. I knew job searching would be difficult because of my image. Even though my resume was good, the tattoos on my hands and neck made it especially difficult.

Numerous people had told me when I was young that I would never find a good job with tattoos. Though I don't necessarily regret getting the tattoos, if I had known then what I know now, I would have been more discreet about their placement. I would have put them just where I could see them.

I was turned down again and again. Nothing was left but to pray and put it in God's hands. I should have done that from day one.

After submitting to God's will, a thought came to mind—the principal at Whitten Middle School. He had told me to contact him when I finished college. I had his card in my wallet the whole time and hadn't thought to call him.

I called him, and he seemed excited to hear from me. He invited me to come for an interview. When I got to the school, the administrators were all very cordial. The principal had already heard me speak, so I didn't have to worry about him judging me.

Long story short, I was hired at Whitten Middle School to work with students exhibiting behavioral issues. It became clear that God had denied me every other job to get me to the one at Whitten. I was sure of it.

I believe that my journey is an example of how God can take the ones least likely to succeed and make them a success. The message is that no matter what a person may have done in life, there's no expiration date on success if he or she looks up instead of at the circumstances.

I am a teacher, motivational speaker, college graduate, and a child of God. I have made it to that place called *success*. Now that I am here, I am motivated to help others find this place. That is, undoubtedly, my next mission.

Therefore, I can say without reservations...I am ready for whatever God has for me.

Allow me to re-introduce myself I am Dr. Tommie Mabry!!!

I have completed my Doctorate Degree from Jackson State University in 2020.

Tommie Mabry's quotes

"You must day dream success, you can't wait till you're sleep to start dreaming."

"If you're not playing the game to beat the game stop playing games."

"I can not walk in my future with my foot in my past."

"It's not an expiration date on success."

"If you let your eyes make your heart decision you'll be mentally blind."

"Push yourself harder than your situation."

"Push me forward don't pull me back."

"Instead of telling me what I can't do, show me what I can do."

A Dark Journey to a light Future the poem.

It took forever to get here. Barefooted on cement, the never-ending dark road provides no light for my path. The rain pours relentlessly, pounding me as I lie down to accept my fate. I walk a few more steps, just mere in chasing the right direction, and the rain turns to snow—I am frozen in place. No ideas come to mind except that I must KEEP GOING. The snow melts in the scorching sun, burning me, torching me as I move toward progress. How much more can I take? My location is etched in my mind, but the roads are many, the obstacles mounting, and I am convinced it is impossible to get there. My body shuts down, but my brain keeps going, a voice unswerving in faith and belief. A slow crawl morphs into an all-out run, a steady pace as I set out to complete the journey ordained for me. Though still fraught with bumps and mountains, and oftentimes finding that I, and not the road, am my fiercest foe, I wallow in trepidation and fear. Still, with all my flaws, I have one motive: KEEP GOING. Suddenly, the bumps become smooth and the mountains move. The view before me is now crystal clear. Even as

I'm basking in the light of where I am, the road of success is never-ending. Still I follow my best and richest advice: KEEP GOING.

Dr. Tommie Mabry

Acknowledgements

Jodi Lea Stewart (Editor)

Carlos D. Smith, Ed.S (Editor)

Whitney Menogan (Editor)

Jackson State University

Tougaloo College

Lawson State

Missouri State University of West Plains

Jackson Public School District